BREWING IN
DORSET

TIM EDGELL AND MIKE BONE

AMBERLEY

First published 2016

Amberley Publishing
The Hill, Stroud
Gloucestershire, GL5 4EP

www.amberley-books.com

ISBN 978 1 4456 5731 8 (print)
ISBN 978 1 4456 5732 5 (ebook)

British Library Cataloguing in Publication Data.
A catalogue record for this book is available from
the British Library.

Typesetting by Amberley Publishing.
Printed in the UK.

Contents

Acknowledgements

Many thanks and cheers to Annie Blick, Barry Brook, Dr Ron Cookson, Andrew Cunningham, Catherine Donne, Hugh and Sue Elmes, Ray Farleigh, Charlie Hathaway, Andy Lane, Chris Marchbanks, George Mortimer, Russell Murfitt, Keith Osborne, Mike Peterson, Jeff Sechiari, Ken Smith, Paul Smith, Dave and Wennona Taylor, Alastair Wallace, Keith Wilson, Kevan Witt, Michael Woodhouse, Jacqui Wragg and to the Dorset brewers and everyone else who has given us help and refreshment along the way.

Andy Lane actively collects Dorset brewery and pub memorabilia. He can be contacted on 07789 275242 or 01308 482132.

For every book sold, the authors will make a donation to cancer charities.

Introduction

Beer has played an important part in the diet, culture and society of Dorset for thousands of years and has been drunk by all ages and all classes of its people and was brewed within the county for most of this time. The introduction provides a brief overview of the brewing process and its history by way of a lead-in to our survey of the county's recent brewing heritage.

Making Beer

Beer was probably discovered, rather than invented, in the Middle East, when cereals became soaked in water and, after subsequent heating, the liquid was fermented by the action of wild yeasts to produce a drink that tasted good with uplifting effects. Trial and error no doubt created some of the earliest beer styles.

Barley is the basis of most European beers and is converted into malt for subsequent use in the brewery. The maltster converts the starch in the barley into a sugar-rich source by partial germination of the barley, steeping it in water, growing the grain on a floor and drying in a kiln to stop further germination. The typical small country

Malthouse at Ansty.

malthouse in Dorset would be worked by one man who would manage a long rectangular growing floor with a steep at one end and a kiln at the other. The house would also need storage space for the grain and the kilned malt and, sometimes, a horse-powered mill to grind malt for sale to home or farm breweries. As breweries increased in size they often chose to make the most of their own malt, and specialist architects designed multi-storey houses with multiple floors and kilns with equipment to move and work the grain.

In the brewery, the malt is first screened and then crushed in a mill to form 'grist'. This is then mixed with hot water – known as 'liquor' – in a mash tun. At this stage the sugars in the malt dissolve to produce sweet, thick liquor or 'wort'. Until the introduction of hops in late medieval times, the wort would be cooled and fermented to become 'ale'. Boiling of the wort with hops in copper was introduced from the Netherlands and gave a bitter taste and a longer life to the beverage. It also produced a much higher yield of wort from a similar quantity of malt used in ale brewing and, after some initial resistance, became a much more popular drink. The new product was known as 'beer', but ale and beer have long since lost their distinctive meanings. The boiled wort would then be cooled and fermented with yeast as before. The beer would now be matured in the cask if it was to be sold as 'real ale' or, if it was to become keg or bottled beer in more-recent times, it would be run into tanks, chilled and filtered to remove any remaining yeasts, then bottled, canned or put under pressure into kegs.

Brewing has remained basically the same over the years but plants have changed radically in size and construction and advances in brewing science have brought about better management of the process.

Early History

Evidence of early brewing in Dorset and elsewhere is scarce. It was probably brought to Dorset by immigrants in Neolithic times and its warming and nourishing qualities were compared favourably to those of wine by Julius Caesar on his brief visit prior to the Roman invasion of Britain. Ale remained the beverage of choice in Anglo-Saxon times when roadside alehouses became the forerunners of the modern pub. The early Christian church also organised 'Church Ales' to raise funds. Documentary evidence becomes more plentiful in the late medieval period. The move from ale to beer and the significant changes that followed the Black Death in the late 1340s was to usher in a major shift from domestic brewing, mainly the responsibility of women, to larger-scale production, the commercialisation of the trade and the rise of the (male) professional brewer.

It is not possible to quantify the extent of domestic brewing in medieval Dorset, but a study of nearby Exeter shows almost three quarters of all households in the late 1370s brewed and sold ale. The Assize of Bread and Ale of 1266 empowered local justices to fix the price of ale in line with that of local wheat and malt and its enforcement, together with a further Assize of 1267 to regulate its sale, created an early licensing regime and some residual records. One example is a claim made in 1280 by the Abbot of Sherborne under the Assize of Beer in Lyme Regis, which raises interesting questions about the supply of ale over some distance, as does a later reference to a dispute over deliveries of ale from the town to the Bishop of Sarum's palace.

Tight controls on brewers and ale sellers continued into the modern era: in Lyme Regis, six common brewers were licensed in 1578 together with the brewer who kept the 'Beer House', presumably a licensed victualler. Elsewhere, Dorchester and Bridport set up municipal brewhouses to control quality and raise revenue for charitable purposes. Poole seems to have been a centre of the trade, regularly importing hops from the Netherlands and shipping both beer and malt to the Channel Islands in the later years of the fifteenth century.

The next two centuries provide some evidence of buildings and plant: the inventories of the Royal Commission on Historic Monuments (RCHM) in Dorset include a malthouse reputed to date from 1580 and a number of references to brewhouses at larger houses. An inventory of 1699 relating to St Giles House, the home of the Earls of Shaftesbury, has a detailed list of equipment in the brewhouse, which included a large and small boiler, two pumps, three coolers, six vats and various smaller items. The malthouse had a lead cistern, a pump, a malt mill, a screen and 'a Hare cloth for the Kill', i.e. a horsehair sheet on which to dry the grain on the floor of the kiln.

Eighteenth Century Expansion

Eighteenth-century brewing history has focused upon the rise of porter as a beer style and an industrial revolution in the big London breweries, but elsewhere about 60 per cent of beer was brewed privately in homes, hospitals, farms, etc., and the rest in pubs and a small number of common breweries. Dorset breweries had to wait until the next century for their industrial revolution, but their beer was to achieve a national reputation in the eighteenth century.

VIEW FROM CHURCH TOWER, BRADFORD ABBAS.

Looking down on the Royal Oak (brewhouse to rear), Bradford Abbas.

In their histories of the county, Cox and Hutchins both identify the war with France that ended in 1714 (i.e. the War of Spanish Succession) as the reason for this recognition of its taste and quality. Imports of French wine had been prohibited during the conflict and bottled provincial beers had become fashionable in London at this time: one contemporary recorded the availability of twenty-three of these in the 1720s, including 'the so much magnified beer of Dorchester'. Dorchester beer received its highest accolade in 1731 when described as 'the finest Malt-liquor in the kingdom, so delicately clean and well tasted'. The brewing and qualities of Dorchester beer feature in many early brewery manuals, such as *The London and Country Brewer* of 1744. The anonymous author of *Everyman his own Brewer* (1768) attributed its particular qualities to use of 'barlies well germinated but not dried to the denomination of malt' and its taste to the 'slackness of the malt, the quantities of salt and wheat flour, mixed with the wort when under fermentation, which gives it a mantling and frothy quality.'

Dorchester beer has been singled out for most comment in contemporary travel journals and early brewing manuals, but its production elsewhere around the county and 'a considerable trade in beer both with Ireland and foreign places' was also noted. Poole continued to export beer and malt, while the importance of the malt trade in Cerne Abbas, Shaftesbury, Dorchester and Blandford also attracted comment. Cerne was even described as 'more famous for beer than any other place in this country' by Bishop Pococke in 1754. Milton Abbas beer was sold in London, Poole and Weymouth prior to the re-siting of the village in 1786.

By 1830 it seems that 'Dorchester beer' had become a generic name for strong brown stout. In his *Town and Country Brewing Book* published that year, William Brande attributed its success to being part-brewed with chalky water, and influenced by the chalk in the soil (presumably in the barley fields) and cellars of the district. He mentions that it was held to be delicious with oysters and cheese. When sent abroad, Brande recommended that corks should be secured with wire and the bottles packed tightly with straw into barrels to prevent losses. He also advised the addition of pound and a quarter of hops to every bushel of malt for beer intended for hot climates.

Survivals of dated maltings such as those at Winterborne Stickland (1767) and Stourton Caundle (1784), and the undated two-storey malthouse at Winterborne Kingston that is typical of this period, suggest that the last part of this century was a time of building or rebuilding maltings. The *Universal British Directory* of the 1790s list twenty-five brewers in eleven towns in the county, seven of whom were also maltsters. Although they do not feature here, Devenish of Weymouth (1742), Hall & Woodhouse of Blandford (1777) and Palmers of Bridport (1794) can date their breweries back to this period.

John Claridge's report to the Board of Agriculture of 1793 aptly summarises progress at the start of another long war with France:

> The growth of barley affords a large produce. A great deal of malt is made for the internal consumption of the county, particularly in the article of strong beer, which is much used. The malt is generally dried with Welch coals. From ten to fourteen bushels of malt per hogshead of sixty-three gallons, with Farnham hops, makes the beer so

much esteemed here, which is kept eighteen months or two years before it is drank; and in some of the towns, ten or twelve thousand bushels of malt are made annually.

Into the Modern Era: The Nineteenth Century

The new century ushered in a golden age for brewers as national production of beer peaked in 1899, but also brought significant change in response to population change, the coming of railways, government regulation and taxation, economic fluctuations and, on the supply side, the availability of new technology and scientific discoveries.

The most significant trend was the dominance of the common or wholesale brewer. County directories list forty-one common brewers in 1823, rising to sixty-one in 1855 and thereafter reducing to twenty-five in the 1898 directory and eighteen in 1911. Most of these are mentioned in the following pages – the survivors were located in the larger towns with the most notable exceptions being the early demise of brewing in Lyme Regis (1860s) and the survival of the country breweries in Milton Abbas and Bere Regis into the inter-war period.

Another useful source for this century is the excise returns to parliament for the Dorset (later Weymouth) collection. The districts in these collections changed frequently and sometimes excluded Dorset towns at the expense of some over the Somerset border. They do, however, include annual returns of the number of common and pub brewers and the quantities of malt used by each category for fifty years after 1831 – these clearly show the changing structure of the trade. While the number of common brewers in the collections remained broadly the same, the proportion of pubs (licensed victuallers) that brewed fell from 40 per cent to 8 per cent. For pubs licensed only to sell beer, the percentage who brewed fell from some 30 per cent to 10 per cent over the same period. Regarding the amount of malt used, the dominance of the common brewers is even more apparent – they used 94 per cent of the malt brewed by all classes of brewer in the year 1880.

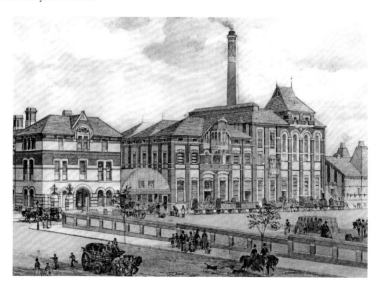

Eldridge Pope's
old brewery,
Dorchester.

The decline of home brewing in this period is harder to estimate as the amount of malt made in the collections over most of this period is not recorded. It is, however, possible to estimate usage by home brewers in the early 1830s as between 40 and 30 per cent of the total used by all classes of brewers. Large houses built or added to at this time often included a brewhouse and the larger farms provided beer as part payment of labourers. Sir James Caird's report on Dorset agriculture in 1850/51 mentions that a gallon a day was provided for workers between the hay and corn harvests, a quart at breakfast (10 a.m.), a pint at 11.30 a.m. for luncheon, a quart during dinner (between 1–2 p.m.), a pint at 4 p.m., 'with something to eat at five' and the rest when work is finished. He estimated the cost of malt on a large farm to be £70 to £80.

The malting industry also underwent significant change. The number of independent maltsters (i.e. excluding the brewers who also made malt) fell from forty-one in 1823 to nine by 1880 and just one in 1903. The drastic decline can best be explained by the decline of home and pub brewing, the end of the tax on malt and the regulation of its manufacture and the decisions of brewers to make their own malt. Many malthouses were located in rural areas and were challenged by static or declining rural population and, after 1875, the onset of agricultural depression.

The Twentieth Century and Beyond

The early years of the last century brought a slowdown in progress and a decline in the number of firms from twenty-three to eighteen between 1903 and 1913. All this was to change in the First World War and the recession that followed. Temperance opposition to brewing, which had had been growing in influence since late Victorian times, was used by David Lloyd George during the war to impose drastic reductions in the strength of beer and licensing hours, together with an experiment in state control of the trade in the Carlisle area. In the end, brewers did quite well financially during the conflict but the long post-war recession saw a decline in per capita consumption to less than half of that in the years before the war. One of the results was a series of mergers and acquisitions, and a further decline in the number of Dorset brewers to ten by 1939.

The temperance assault had diminished by the start of the Second World War, but brewers suffered from shortage of materials and enemy damage to its breweries and tied estate. Consumption was to rise again in the 1960s as the economy recovered and continuing population growth to the east of the county, particularly in the Bournemouth and Poole area, boosted demand. Bournemouth and Christchurch were to join Dorset as part of the local government reforms of 1974.

The return of good times did not, however, protect Dorset's brewers from the need to adapt as consumer preferences, competition and government regulation posed fresh challenges. The 1960s saw the growth in sales of keg beers and national brands, such as Watney's Red Barrel, that were widely advertised, as well as a preference to drinking at home from bottles and cans bought at supermarkets. Dorset brewers, who had adapted well to the change in taste from strong ales to lighter Burton-style bitters in the nineteenth century, now faced the challenge posed by lager. This continental beer style was first introduced with little success into the UK in the late nineteenth century

6D Mild pump clip,
Sixpenny Brewery.

but came to dominate the beer market in the later twentieth century, its share of beer sales rising from 1 per cent in 1960 to 50 per cent by 1989.

Perhaps the most significant challenge to Dorset brewers was the 'merger mania' in the years up to 1980 and the government's reaction to a perceived threat to competition. The report of the Monopolies & Mergers Commission and the subsequent Beer Orders set in motion another series of changes that were to result in the loss of Dorset's largest breweries in Weymouth and Dorchester. At the time of writing, the agreement of AB Inbev and SABMiller to merge has created the first global brewer with a number of heavily advertised lager brands. The rise of lager now seems to have come to a halt and there has been a small revival of ale. The latter is due to some extent by the rise of the micro, or craft, brewery movement, which began in the UK in the 1970s and, with their focus on quality and diversity, have opened the latest chapter in Dorset brewery history.

The framework of the book is provided by the excellent Brewery History Society publication *A Century of British Brewers* by Norman Barber. The structure then follows a geographical path, zig-zagging northwards across the chapters from east to west like an old typewriter in reverse.

East Dorset

Stanpit sees the start of a Dorset brewing odyssey through the past and present. Located in the far east of Dorset, when the Stanpit Brewery traded it was in Hampshire. Despite being a small place, Stanpit had two breweries a couple of hundred yards apart in the nineteenth century. The Stanpit Brewery, at numbers 92–106, had existed for decades when it was acquired by Charles Absolom of Fordingbridge in 1886. Brewing ceased around 1900, and the extended house still stands.

Further up the road at numbers 56–64, the Victoria Steam Brewery was set up around 1870 by Henry Laurence. It was adjacent to the Ship in Distress, a renowned smugglers' pub. Under new owners, Alfred and Henry Youngman, the name was changed to the Avon Brewery in 1894. However, in 1897, the Avon Brewery was acquired by Crowleys of Alton. Most of the buildings survive as housing.

Next on the journey is Christchurch and, at 11 High Street, the Steam Brewery. The tower of the Steam Brewery, which bore the large inscription 'Aldridge & Co. Brewery Est. 1783', was a landmark in the town for years. By 1906, Aldridge & Co. were bankrupt and in 1907 the business was acquired by Frampton Brothers, who until then had brewed in Pokesdown.

The Stanpit Brewery. (Copyright The Red House Museum)

Left: The Ship in Distress, Stanpit.

Right: Advert for Frampton Bros, Christchurch.

Frampton Brothers continued to brew at the Steam Brewery until 1934, when the brewery was sold to Hammertons of London. In November 1956, the old tower was demolished for safety reasons. The brewery was then owned by Watneys of London, who had acquired Hammertons in 1951.

John King brewed further down the High Street at the Christchurch Brewery, which is where the Arcado Lounge now stands. The old brewery stood next to the Square House, a Georgian mansion built around 1776 by John Cook. His family had been brewing in Christchurch since the early eighteenth century. The King family continued to brew at the Christchurch Brewery until it was acquired by Strongs of Romsey in 1891.

Just north of Christchurch at Bockhampton, there was a small, short-lived brewery that began brewing in 1991. The Cook Brewery Co. supplied beers such as Priory 900 and New Forest Gold in casks and bottles, but brewed their last pint in 1995.

Across to Southbourne and to the present day, Jennifer Tingay launched Southbourne Brewing Ltd in 2013. She brewed her first beer, Paddler, on New Year's Eve. Using spare capacity at the Lyme Regis Brewery, Jennifer has already won awards both for her brewery and for her oatmeal stout, Stroller. Now, via investment from crowd funding, the production of Southbourne ales will transfer to a new brewery and bar on Poole Hill, in what used to be the Bumbles nightclub. Jennifer is looking forward excitedly to opening day and to adding a new tourist destination to this part of Dorset.

A short hop away in Pokesdown, the original New Bell Inn was built in the 1850s as the town began to expand. It had a brewhouse to the rear. The inn was rebuilt in 1904 and, around 1908, was acquired by Frampton Brothers.

In 1902, Frampton Brothers had also acquired the Pokesdown Brewery before moving their operations to Christchurch in 1907. The Pokesdown Brewery at

Above left: Brewery tower after take over by Hammertons. (Copyright The Red House Museum)

Above right: Stoneware flagon for John King, Christchurch Brewery.

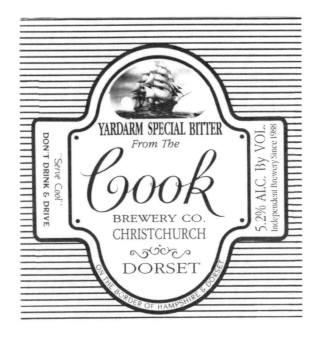

Beer label for Cook's Brewery, Christchurch.

Jennifer Tingay of Southbourne Ales.

Advert for Southbourne Ales.

The New Bell Inn, Pokesdown.

27 Southbourne Road had been built in 1873 by Emmanuel Watton. He ran the brewery until his death, when he was succeeded by his widow Elizabeth.

Moving on to Bournemouth, the Bournemouth Brewery was established at 117 Holdenhurst Road, behind the Railway Hotel, in 1868. The brewery passed through several owners and was registered as Crane & Osmond Ltd in 1898. It then passed through several more owners, including a Hilda Ogden, until it was acquired by Strongs of Romsey in 1925. Thenceforth it was used as a depot until, in 1973, the site was cleared. An office block, Waverley House, now stands in place of the old brewery.

The Tapps Arms was built in a remote spot on heath land in 1809, on what is now Old Christchurch Road. The inn was remodelled in 1812 when owned by the Tregonwell family. Renamed the Tregonwell Arms, it was Bournemouth's first inn and brewhouse. Sadly, this lovely old pub was demolished in 1885.

Winding forward 110 years, the Firefly & Firkin at 38 Holdenhurst Road commenced brewing in 1995. Their beers, such as Glow Worm and Lightning Bug, proved popular, but brewing ceased in 1999. The Stonegate Pub Co. became new

Watton's Brewery, Pokesdown.

The Bournemouth Brewery.

Bournemouth Brewery dray at the Blackwater Ferry, Hurn.

The Tregonwell Arms, Bournemouth.

Beermat for the Firefly & Firkin, Bournemouth.

owners of the premises and renamed the pub The Inferno. With help from Salisbury Brewery, brewing recommenced in 2014 and a beer, Dorset Screamer, was produced. However the venture was short-lived and the on-site microbrewery is waiting for another brewer to come along.

Over in Poole, the Dolphin Brewery was the largest of Poole's former breweries. Reputedly founded by the Strong family at the pub of this name in 1745, it passed through a number of hands until Tom Rickman's bankruptcy in 1864, when it was a fifteen-quarter steam-powered plant with two malthouses, one of which later passed to Christopher Hill. John Taylor Marston became sole owner in 1878 and incorporated as Marston's Dolphin Brewery Ltd in 1897 with fifty-nine pubs. The brewery was taken over by Strong & Co. of Romsey in 1926 and survived as a depot until 1939.

The Poole Brewery was founded by Joseph King in 1795 and moved to a new brewery in 1818. King's sons expanded the business and purchased two breweries in Christchurch. After their deaths in 1852 the business passed to a partnership that included Frederick Styring, a local farmer who was soon to become its sole owner. In 1881, George Pope, a brother of Alfred and Edwin of the Dorchester Brewery, and Robert Walmersley took over until Styring & Co. was taken over by Eldridge, Pope & Co. Ltd in 1900. The Towngate site continued in use until the maltings closed in the 1950s.

David Rawlins set up the new Poole Brewery in an old engineering workshop on Sterte Avenue in 1981. He then purchased The Brewhouse pub in the high street and began brewing there in a small brewhouse behind the pub. Production was wholly transferred to The Brewhouse site in 1987, when the premises in Sterte Avenue closed.

Letterhead for the Dolphin Brewery, Poole.

Right: Beer label for Marston's Brewery, Poole.

Below: Styring's Brewery, Poole. (Courtesy of Brewery History Society)

Above left: Advert for Styring's Brewery.

Above right: Poole Brewery branding.

Brewhouse at The Brewhouse, Poole. (Courtesy of Brewery History Society)

In 2002, The Brewhouse was sold to the Milk Street Brewery of Frome. Soon after, the brewhouse behind the pub was demolished to be replaced by a small block of flats called The Old Brewery.

At this point, mention must be made of the Brewhouse & Kitchen pub in Dear Hay Lane. The pub is part of the Brewhouse & Kitchen chain, which will be opening two more pubs in Bournemouth and Southbourne in 2016. The Brewhouse & Kitchen in Dorchester is looked at in more detail in chapter five.

Also in Poole, in Abingdon Road, is the Bournemouth Brewing Co. Set up in 2013 by Chris Mathers with help from his family, who have been involved in brewing on and off since 1928, the brewery has gone from strength to strength. First there was larger kit, then a move to larger premises, and then the installation of a distillery and the launch of Dorset Smugglers Vodka. In 2015, the brewery opened its first pub, the Smuggler's Run, in Parkstone, and will follow that up with the opening of a second pub in Ashley Cross in 2016.

Heading north, in the nineteenth century and into the twentieth century, Wimborne had two main breweries: Ellis' Town Brewery and Habgood's Julian Brewery. The Town Brewery in Mill Lane lasted over a century, from its opening in the mid-1820s to when it was sold to Hall & Woodhouse in 1937 along with eighteen pubs.

The Julian Brewery was located behind what is now the Minster Arms. Back then the pub was called the Three Lions, and the landlord Joseph Piddle brewed in the yard from the 1840s. George Habgood acquired the pub in the 1860s and built the Julian Brewery in 1876. However, in 1915, the brewery and seventeen pubs were sold to Groves of Weymouth.

Sandbanks Bitter pump clip,
Bournemouth Brewing Co.

The Smuggler's Run, Parkstone.

Letterhead for Ellis' Brewery, Wimborne.

Beer label for Habgood's Brewery, Wimborne.

After a gap of almost eighty years, brewing has made a very welcome return to Wimborne. Named after the number of arches under Julian's Bridge to the west of the town, Steve Farrell started brewing at the Eight Arch Brewing Co. in early 2015. Steve's aim is to embrace the new wave of brewing with a wide variety of hops and ingredients to create flavoursome ales. His beers, such as Parabolic Pale and Corbel, are available in an increasing number of pubs and outlets, or at the brewery bar in Stone Lane.

The fortunate residents of Wimborne have now gained a second brewery within a year. Late in 2015, Adam Bascombe launched The Brew Shack in Leigh Road. Friends called Adam's shed, where he had his homebrew kit, the brew shack, so Adam continued with the name. His aim is to brew handmade, small-batch beers using locally sourced ingredients. He stresses that the brewery is very adaptable and that new recipes will be developed in response to customer feedback. There is also a brewery bar which serves already popular beers such as English Pale Ale and Black Lane Stout.

Set in the heart of the north-east Dorset countryside, Scott Wayland established the Sixpenny Brewery in 2009 at Sixpenny Handley. Since then, his beers have won multiple awards. In 2015, the Sixpenny Brewery was voted Best Brewer in the Taste of Dorset Awards. Congratulations.

Attached to the brewery, The Sixpenny Tap lays claim to being the smallest pub in Britain. Not held back by its cosy size, The Sixpenny Tap is a regular entry in the *CAMRA's Good Beer Guide*. Sixpenny beers are available there in cask, bottle and from an 'honesty tap' installed on the front of the bar.

Across to Cranborne and the Sheaf of Arrows pub that in the 1990s was home to the Cranborne Brewery. The brewery was located in the yard behind the pub in an outbuilding to the right with a central roof dormer. John and Kate Tuppen started the Cranborne Brewery with assistance from Graham Moss, and brewed its first ever brew on 12 March 1996. However, it proved to be a short-lived venture, and the brewery closed in 1998 after a change of ownership.

Eight Arch Brewery bottles, Wimborne.

Left: Bowstring Bitter pump clip, Eight Arch Brewery.

Below: Interior of The Brew Shack, Wimborne.

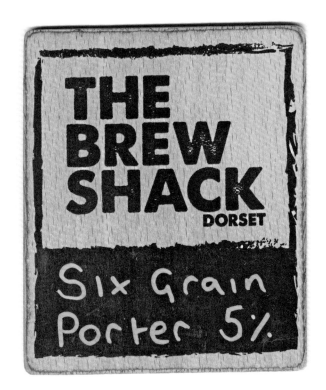

Right: Six Grain Porter
pump clip, The Brew Shack.

Below: Scott Wayland
and Kevin Patrick at The
Sixpenny Tap, Sixpenny
Handley.

Display of Sixpenny Brewery's award-winning ales.

Cranborne Brewery (top centre) at the Sheaf of Arrows.

Cranborne Brewery bottle, glass and jug.

Purbeck Area

On the Isle of Purbeck, a brewery was established at Swanage in the eighteenth century. Then owned by the Edmunds family, they sold it to Henry Gillingham in 1804. Henry's son, Henry junior, sold the brewery to the Earl of Eldon in 1849, then being leased to James Panton of Wareham. Following a catastrophic fire in 1854, which left only the walls standing, the brewery was rebuilt and continued to brew the renowned Swanage Pale Ale using water from its own pure spring. In 1893, the brewery was acquired by Strongs of Romsey, and was demolished in 1899. The site is now the health centre.

After a gap of over a century, Swanage now has new brewers in the shape of Hattie Browns Brewery. Kevin Hunt and Jean Young named their brewery after their dog, and have spent several years converting an old slaughterhouse into a much better use. Using some of the kit from the old Tom Brown's Brewery in Dorchester, and after many test brews, Moonlite was launched in 2015. Moonlite will be followed by other beers in 2016. Hattie Browns beer is available at the classic Square and Compass pub at Worth Matravers.

Panton's Brewery, Swanage.

The Royal Oak, Herston (an old Swanage Brewery pub).

Hattie Browns Brewery.

Moonlite pump clip, Hattie Browns.

Just outside Swanage, the road forks. The first building on the right on the road to Langton Matravers is Coombe Farm. Just behind the farmhouse is a listed barn with a central hipped roof and turret. To the right of this is a former brewery, which was started in the 1860s by William Edmunds. The family carried on the brewery until it was acquired by Pantons of Wareham in 1892. Further on in Langton Matravers, the Old Malthouse is now a school. In the late nineteenth century, census returns show Charles Chinchen Edmunds occupying the premises.

At Corfe Castle, at the heart of Purbeck, it seems that beer was brewed at all of the inns at one time or another in the nineteenth century. Looking down at the Greyhound Inn from the church tower, there was a small brewhouse in the outbuildings to the rear. To the right of the Castle Inn, beer was brewed in the adjoining property until it was acquired by Pantons of Wareham.

Brewing has since returned to Corfe Castle, or, to be more accurate, to a farm nearby. In 2011, Steve and Chris Millar launched their family concern, the Corfe Castle Brewery. At first, only bottled ales were produced, as brewing was interrupted by bats – who roosted in the outbuilding that was converted to the brewhouse. The aim of the brewery is to use natural ingredients with the least possible exposure to chemical additives. The brewery was soon able to supply casks of their beer to local pubs and beer festivals, along with their core range of bottled beer.

Edmunds' Brewery (right of tower), Langton Matravers.

The Old Malthouse, Langton Matravers.

Looking down on the Greyhound Inn, Corfe Castle.

Brewhouse next to the Castle Inn, Corfe Castle.

Steve and Chris Millar of the Corfe Castle Brewery.

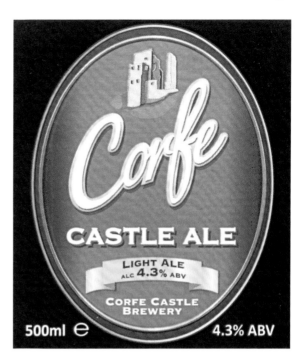

Beer label for the Corfe Castle Brewery.

Looking out over the beautiful Studland Bay, the Bankes Arms has another reason to be cheerful: it has its own brewery next door. The Isle of Purbeck Brewery was started in 2003 by the Lightbown family, who own the Bankes Arms. The names of their beers, such as Fossil Fuel and Jurassic Joule, are inspired by local themes. It is always a pleasure to visit the Bankes Arms and encounter an array of Isle of Purbeck Brewery beers on the hand pumps, or at their ever-popular summer beer festival.

Moving across Purbeck, in the nineteenth century, the Weld Arms at East Lulworth brewed beer for the Weld Estate in a small brewhouse to the rear. The pub was then leased to Groves of Weymouth in 1895, and subsequently became a Devenish house.

While in Purbeck, a special mention needs to be made of the Dead Brewers Society, run by beer aficionado Alastair Wallace. The society is an organisation of retired brewers who seek out and find every brewing specification of old beers. The former dead beers are then recreated with the help of new microbreweries to give them a bit of history. The society recently resurrected the old Panton's Family Ale, which was true to its original style and brewed by Mighty Hop of Lyme Regis.

To the left of Wareham Bridge on Abbots Quay stood the brewery and malthouse premises that were founded in 1823 by Stephen White. Around 1830, Stephen Bennett acquired the business. It remained in the hands of the Bennett family until 1906, when it was sold to Strongs of Romsey along with eleven pubs. The malthouse remains today as housing.

The Sawpit Brewery and malthouse also comes into view at the top centre of the aerial photograph on page 33. Set up by the Panton family in the early nineteenth century, the malthouse was still used for nearly half a century after Pantons moved their brewing operations to Pound Lane.

The Bankes Arms,
Studland.

Isle of Purbeck
Brewery ales at the
Bankes Arms bar.

The Weld Arms, East
Lulworth.

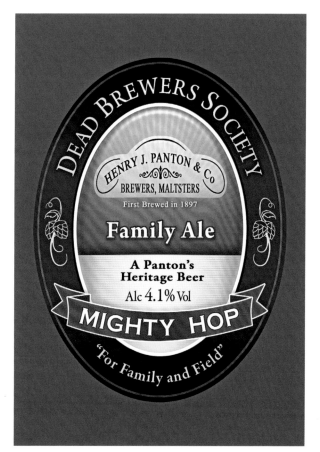

Right: Panton's Family Ale pump clip, Dead Brewers Society.

Below: Bennett's Brewery (lower left), Wareham.

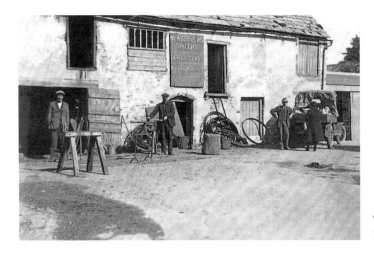

The old Sawpits
Brewery, Wareham.

The brewery in Pound Lane had been established by the Phippard family, who also owned four inns, by 1818. In the early 1820s, Samuel Townsend acquired the brewery, and, in turn, in the early 1840s it was acquired by James Panton, who had been brewing at Sawpits. Under James Panton, the concern expanded, taking on the Swanage Brewery in the late 1840s and Veals of Ringwood in 1870. Brewing continued at the three sites until Henry John Panton & Co. was acquired by Strongs of Romsey in 1892.

In north-west Purbeck, Bere Regis had a brewery for over 150 years. Located to the left of the photograph on page 35 just in front of the church, it was re-established around 1830 by John Casher at the end of the gardens of the Royal Oak pub. The brewery went through a succession of owners and ended up in the hands of Johnson & Tozer. The business was sold to Strongs of Romsey in 1921, and the brewery was demolished in 1923, to be replaced by houses. Thankfully, the Royal Oak still serves thirst-quenching ale.

Panton's Brewery
staff, Wareham.

Right: The old Panton's Brewery, Wareham.

Below: Bere Regis Brewery (in front of the church).

THE CROSS, BERE REGIS.

The Royal Oak, Bere Regis.

Blandford to Bourton

Setting off again, now in Winterborne Kingston, the first brewery encountered is that of the Sunny Republic Brewing Co. Launched in 2012 by Brent and Rosie Smith, who wanted the name of their brewery to sound bright and upbeat, Sunny Republic is located in wonderful converted Georgian barns. The brewing kit is ultra-modern and reflects the type of beers Sunny Republic is producing. Beers such as Beach Blonde and Dune Raider are full of flavour and are brewed with an innovative mix of malt and hops. Go to the Friday night brewery bar for a sample.

The Sunny Republic Brewing Co., Winterborne Kingston.

Huna Red pump clip,
Sunny Republic.

The hilly and remote region between Blandford and Ansty is an unlikely birthplace for Dorset's largest surviving brewery, Hall & Woodhouse. Their history begins with the Hall family of Dewlish, where William Hall was brewing by 1770 – our first record of this concern. After his death in 1782 the business passed to his son Thomas and, in 1842, to his nephew Charles. Charles decided to sell the business and it passed to local farmer William Symes in 1843, who brewed here until 1859, when a disastrous fire destroyed the brewery and much of the village. In the two photographic views of Dewlish seen on page 39, opposite the chapel and Old Parsonage Farmhouse, walls survive that are not there today. These are probably the remains of the brewery, for it was on that site. The location is marked now by a palm tree.

Nearby, the Milton Brewery in Milton Abbas, whose beers are noted in the introduction, was relocated to its present site when the old village was removed as part of the landscaping plans of the owner of the estate in the 1780s. Brewers after this included John Ham (from 1786), John Warne (from 1842) and then the Fookes family (from about 1850), who remained here until it became the last business taken over by Groves of Weymouth in 1950. This classic farm brewery shown in the evocative illustration was powered by a horse mill in 1850 and was maintained as a museum until converted into housing in the 1980s.

A short distance away, the brewery at Ansty in Hilton began in 1777 when Charles Hall, son of William, left Dewlish to establish a closely related family business here. The new brewery grew steadily, supplying the military in Weymouth during the wars with France, and passed to Charles's son Robert on his death in 1827. Robert had no children and the business passed to G. E. (Edward) Woodhouse, a former employee and partner who had married into the family, in 1858. The Woodhouse family have remained in control of Hall & Woodhouse ever since.

View of the
Dewlish Brewery
site (centre).

Alternative view
of the Dewlish
Brewery site
(centre).

Fookes Bros Brewery, Milton Abbas.

Left: Beer bottles from Henry Fookes.

Below: Ansty Brewery.

ANSTY BREWERY, FROM THE BLANDFORD ROAD.

The business, run in conjunction with a farm, made use of local barley, Kentish hops and brewing water from Melcombe Horsey Hill, but was conducted on a different scale from that at Milton Abbas. The head brewer at the time of Alfred Barnard's (a noted brewery historian) visit to Ansty in 1890 was a pupil of Frank Faulkner, author of well-known brewing textbooks, and the plant was rebuilt and re-equipped to meet the expanding trade that followed purchases after 1860 of a number of small breweries in Dorchester, Lychett Minster and Hazelbury Bryan. Brewing finished at Ansty in the early 1900s, but the site was to remain in use until 1937. Malting continued here until about 1940 and the great malthouse remains today as the village hall. Much else has gone but Broad Close, the old Woodhouse residence, is now the popular Fox Inn.

Close by, the hamlet of Melcombe Horsey is now known as Higher Melcombe. Details of the Melcombe Horsey Brewery are patchy, but the chapel of the magnificent manor house was divided into two storeys in the late eighteenth century and contained a brewhouse. The Melcombe Horsey Brewery was acquired by Hall & Woodhouse around 1900 and, during renovations fifty years later, a substantial chimney was removed which passed through one of the chapel's blocked up windows.

Back across to Blandford St Mary, the home today of Hall & Woodhouse. The remote but delightful location of the Ansty brewery was not best suited to the business and the purchase of the Blandford St Mary Brewery from Neame & Cock in 1883 began the slow process of relocation to a site that was close to the Somerset & Dorset Railway. Known as Hector's Brewery after a previous owner, the sale details of the business included a nine-quarter steam-driven plant, the brewery house and other buildings at Blandford, two maltings at Winterborne Stickland and fifteen tied houses, some as far away as Southampton. The purchase was clearly a risk: annual turnover averaged only £10,000 at a time of 'unprecedented agricultural distress', as the sale details put it, but under new management the business continued to prosper.

The old Ansty Brewery malthouses.

Advert for Hall & Woodhouse, Ansty and Blandford.

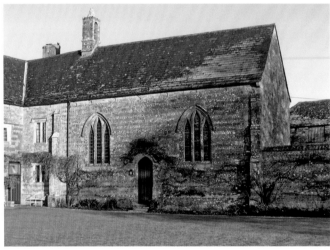

Probably the old Melcombe Horsey Brewery.

Hector's Brewery, Blandford St Mary.

At the time of Alfred Barnard's visit to Hall & Woodhouse, some thirty people were employed at Blandford and forty at Ansty. The company owned upwards of fifty tied houses and had over 5,000 customers on the books. Barnard duly sampled the beers, with a particular appreciation of the XXXX old October – the verdict was 'simply perfection'.

In 1898, a limited company was registered to include the businesses conducted at Ansty and Blandford, plus that of the Godwin Brothers in Durweston. The old Blandford Brewery had been extended in the years before this with the addition of a fine sixty-quarter malthouse, but work on the new 'ornamental' brewery to rival the design of Pope's in Dorchester was begun in 1898 to the designs of Arthur Kinder of London. The first brew here took place in 1900, the same year Hector's Brewery burnt down.

For Hall & Woodhouse, the new century brought further purchases of breweries and tied houses and expansion in the wine and spirits and off-licence trade. The breweries and houses acquired included those at Melcombe Horsey, Fontmell Magna, Wimborne and, after much negotiation, the long-coveted business of Matthews of Gillingham in 1963. The company now owned some 200 tied houses and forty off-licences. Concentration on the free and take-home trade, soft drinks manufacture, a conservative financial strategy and a commitment to independence brought survival into the twenty-first century with the acquisition of King & Barnes of Horsham in 2002 and the opening of their new brewery in June 2012.

Hall & Woodhouse's Brewery, Blandford St Mary.

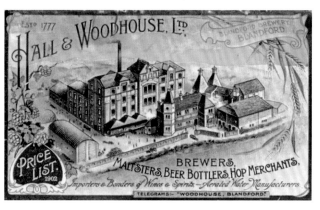

Advert for Hall & Woodhouse showing the brewery.

Above: Advert for Hall & Woodhouse showing the early badger trademark.

Left: Advert for Badger Beers.

Above: Opening of Hall &
Woodhouse's new brewery.

Right: Welcome to Badger Country
at the Half Moon, Shaftesbury.

Pub sign at the Halfway Inn, Norden.

Across the River Stour, the frontage of the listed Crown Hotel was rebuilt in the Georgian style in the last century, but this old coaching inn is thought to be one of the oldest hostelries in Dorset, dating back to the fifteenth century. The busy London – Exeter route was of great importance to Blandford's economy and inns brewed their own beer – only one common brewer claimed for losses after the Great Fire of Blandford in 1731. The Crown's brewhouse was to the rear of the hotel. George Jones, its last landlord before the sale to Hall & Woodhouse in 1931, also supplied beer to the nearby Portman estate.

Blandford's Town Brewery was to remain independent until sold to Simonds of Reading in 1939 with eight pubs. The brewery was founded in King's Arms Yard, White Cliff Mill Street, after 1731 and by 1859 was operated by John Lewis. By 1880, it had passed to John Lewis Marsh, a relative who rebuilt the brewery and malthouse, the company becoming J. L. Marsh and Sons Ltd in 1912. Their 'Pure Malt and Hop Ales' won prizes and were popular locally. The Bryanston Street buildings were seen as a nuisance by the mid-1980s and demolished in 1986.

Several miles north-west of Blandford, much of the old Durweston Brewery remains even though it closed over a century ago. Established in 1753, it stayed in the hands of the Godwin family until Henry Godwin retired in 1898 and it was sold to Hall & Woodhouse along with twenty-six pubs.

The Crown Hotel,
Blandford Forum.

Through the arch of
the Crown Hotel.

Marsh's Brewery,
Blandford Forum.

Left: Advert for Marsh's Brewery.

Below: The old Durweston Brewery.

A few miles further on, the village of Shroton (or Iwerne Courtney) had a brewery for most of the nineteenth century. It passed through the ownership of Edwin Andrews, Charles Godwin and Alfred Packard before being sold to Sibeth Brothers of Fontmell Magna in 1889 along with six pubs. The brewery stood approximately where the northern terrace of The Laurels is now.

A little further west, the Fiddleford Inn was previously called the Travellers Rest. The Adams family brewed at the pub from the mid-nineteenth century until it closed in 1903. Brewing took place at the rear, with access through an arch, which is now filled in but still evident on the front of the pub.

Built in 1708, the White Hart at Sturminster Newton was a brew pub for around 200 years. Latterly, Harry Richard Chapman was the landlord and brewer, but he sold the inn to Hall & Woodhouse in around 1910 and brewing ceased.

The Fontmell Magna Brewery transferred to the present site in 1828, when it was owned by local farmer, brewer and maltster William Monkton. On his death in 1875, it passed to his cousin George Flower. It is an impressive survival of a small country brewery that was modernised by Pontifex of London to the highest standards of the time. J. W. Flower had trained as a brewer in Weymouth but sold the business to A. F. T. Sibeth when he set up an engineering business. The business was auctioned in 1904 with twenty tied houses, but the brewery did not meet its reserve price. Most of the brewery frontage remains today.

Across to Marnhull, where the old Marnhull Brewery still stands. Now the local landmark is without its chimney and the left-hand portion of the building. Founded by 1821, the brewery went through a succession of owners until Eldridge Pope acquired it from Jennings, Styring, White & Co. in 1913 along with thirty-six pubs.

From around 1850, the Parnham family brewed in buildings at what is now Hingarston House. Known as the Walton Elm Brewery, John Parnham & Co. was acquired by the Marnhull Brewery in 1897 with two pubs.

Stoneware flagon for A. Packard & Co., Shroton Brewery.

The Fiddleford Inn (formerly the Traveller's Rest).

The White Hart, Sturminster Newton.

The Crown Brewery, Fontmell Magna.

The old Crown Brewery.

Brewery Hill (side of brewery through trees), Marnhull.

Letterhead for John Parnham's Brewery, Marnhull.

On to Shaftesbury, the last refuge of small brewers in Dorset. During the nineteenth century, there were at least a dozen pub brewers and several more small-scale brewers. One such pub was the Two Brewers Inn, which is still in St James Street. The pub's name probably refers to travelling brewers who touted their ale to inns before the tied house arrangement.

The Kings Arms in Bleke Street was another brew pub. Joseph Lush, W. Sawyer and George Williams all brewed at the pub before it was sold to R. W. Borley of the Grosvenor Brewery in 1876.

The Grosvenor Hotel, Shaftesbury's premier town centre establishment, also had a brewery in buildings to the rear. In 1887, the premises were acquired by Robert William Borley, who a short time later appointed Robert Upcroft as brewer at the Grosvenor Brewery. R. W. Borley is listed as a brewer in directories until 1915. E. Browning continued to brew until the 1920s when their five pubs were sold to Matthews of Gillingham and Hall & Woodhouse, and brewing ceased.

Up on the western edge of Gillingham, the Wyke Brewery was started by the Matthews family of nearby Milton, where Thomas was the major landowner. His brothers, Harry and Joseph, had started in business by 1840 and had an 'extensive brewery' by 1848. This was further developed by Thomas's son, George Blandford Matthews, who added a malting to his Purns Mill and rebuilt the brewery around 1860. A substantial tied estate was acquired in north Dorset and Somerset by his successors George Gerrard and Gerrard Blandford Matthews, with accommodation for brewery workers. Hall & Woodhouse took over the business in 1963 after years of negotiation and brewing ceased.

The Two Brewers Inn (left), Shaftesbury.

Tankard for George Williams, Kings Arms, Shaftesbury.

The Grosvenor Hotel, Shaftesbury.

Beer label for R. W. Borley, Grosvenor Hotel.

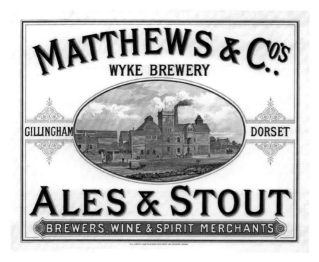

Advert for Matthews & Co., Wyke Brewery, Gillingham.

The old Wyke Brewery.

A barrel roll away from the old Wyke Brewery, Paul Smith started Small Paul's Brewery in 2006. Despite being a nanobrewery, Small Paul produces beer of such consistently high quality that he has taken on the larger breweries and won several prestigious beer festivals. In 2010, his beer Elder Sarum triumphed at the Weymouth Octoberfest, and in 2013 Chocolate Porter was voted beer of the festival at Dorchester Beerex. Although he only brews four firkins a month on average, Small Paul has constant demand for his beer from over twenty pubs.

On to the northernmost pub in Dorset, the White Lion Inn at Bourton. In the nineteenth century, the White Lion was a brew pub. The Ing family brewed there from around 1860 to the 1890s, when the pub was acquired by Frome United Breweries.

Over to the northernmost brewery in Dorset, albeit only an occasional brewery. Down the road from the White Lion, King Alfred Ales is another nanobrewery that appears in *CAMRA's Good Beer Guide*. Although infrequent, King Alfred's beer has made several welcome appearances at the White Lion Inn.

Above: Paul Smith of Small Paul's
Brewery, Gillingham.

Right: Invicta pump clip, Small
Paul's.

Above: The White Horse Inn, Bourton.

Left: Saxon Gold pump clip, King Alfred Ales.

Portland and Weymouth Area

On the distinctive Isle of Portland, there was a short-lived brewery in the late nineteenth century next door to the old Kings Arms pub at 88 Chiswell. Thomas Comden was at the Kings Arms by 1877, but details about his Chesil Brewery are sketchy. Comden had gone from the Kings Arms by 1885, and the pub was in the hands of Groves of Weymouth by 1895. The old Kings Arms is now a private house, but the plaque from Groves Brewery is still there and has recently been restored.

Over in Weymouth, the surviving buildings in and around the Brewers Quay development constitute a superb brewery landscape with the Hope Brewery as its star attraction. This business was started in 1840 by Levi Groves, son of John Groves of Puncknowle in west Dorset. His son John took over the business in 1854 and grew it by acquisition of a number of pubs and small breweries in the local area between 1877 and his death in 1905. These included breweries in Wyke Regis, Melcombe Regis, Maiden Newton, East Burton, Martinstown, Dorchester (the Phoenix Brewery), Portland and Sydling St. Nicholas. Some of these had previously taken over other small concerns, as mentioned elsewhere in this book.

The old Kings Arms, Portland.

Detail of the Groves plaque
on the old Kings Arms.

The Hope brewery,
Weymouth.

The business was incorporated as John Groves & Sons Ltd in 1895 and commissioned a leading brewers' architect, Arthur Kinder, to build an 'ornamental' brewery that was completed in 1904. John Groves, who was knighted in 1900, is a good example of how successful brewers could rise in society and local politics. The report of his knighthood in the *Southern Times* recorded his service to Weymouth as magistrate, mayor, alderman and councillor, and his benevolence – which included the gift of the Sidney Hall as a memorial to his youngest son.

His son Herbert added Wimborne's Julian Brewery to its acquisitions in 1915 but faced similar difficulties to other brewers during the First World War and the recession that followed. Shortages of materials were such that their great rivals Devenish even considered amalgamating with them. The idea came to nothing as trade gradually revived. The Devenish Brewery was badly damaged by bombing in 1940 and arrangements were made with Eldridge Pope and Groves to brew for them at cost, plus a charge for overhead expenses. On rebuilding in 1942, Devenish presented Groves and Popes with silver salvers by way of appreciation, but the bitter business rivalry between the neighbouring businesses resumed 'with all the intensity it had exhibited before the first bombs dropped'. Military activity at the Portland naval base and preparation for the D-Day landings, however, boosted trade for both.

Proposed design for
the Groves Brewery,
Weymouth.

Advert for John Groves &
Sons.

Beermat showing Groves
branding.

J. Groves leaded windows at the Giant Inn, Cerne Abbas.

Groves made their final Dorset acquisition in 1950 when they took over the historic Milton Abbas Brewery, with six pubs, but eventually fell victim to merger mania when purchased by Devenish in 1960. The Hope Brewery is currently up for redevelopment but its listed status should protect it as a fine monument to Dorset's brewing heritage.

The Weymouth or Devenish Brewery claimed to be one of the oldest in continuous production prior to its closure in the 1980s. In 1742, Mary Fowler leased a stable and a plot that was the site of an old brewhouse. She subsequently built a new one before the business passed to her son-in-law, John Flew, by the 1770s. It was then leased to William Devenish in 1821 and purchased in 1824. Still called the Flew Brewery in Devenish's early years, the small brewery shown in the illustration was one of three at work in the square in the early years of this century.

William made numerous additions as trade grew and it became J. A. Devenish & Co. in 1851 after William's partner James Aldridge Devenish took over. By 1892, they had acquired the largest share of pubs in the Weymouth and Dorchester borough licensing districts and had developed a substantial trade in the Channel Islands. A maritime connection also brought some royal warrants after Devenish were commanded to supply a case of their pale ale to the future King Edward VII when the royal yacht called at Weymouth in 1872. Four more followed later. The company was incorporated in 1889 as J. A. Devenish & Co. Ltd.

After the First World War the company embarked upon a strategy of expansion in the west that was to lead to its status as a regional brewer. In 1921 they took over Carne's Falmouth Brewery, followed by takeovers of Aylwin & Sowden's Well Park Brewery in Exeter (1925), the Redruth Brewery Co. Ltd (1934), Vallance's Brewery in Sidmouth (1957) and great rivals John Groves & Sons Ltd in 1960.

The brewery was badly damaged in the Second World War and its appearance somewhat changed in the rebuilding. After the war, the range of beers was extended, kegs introduced, the home trade developed and prizes were won at exhibitions, but concerns for the future of the brewery hovered in these years of merger mania, especially when Devenish came under the 'Whitbread umbrella'. Events moved quickly in the mid-1980s as first the Weymouth Brewery was closed in 1985 as production was

Brewers Quay, Weymouth.

The old Groves maltings.

Beer label for Devenish & Groves Ltd.

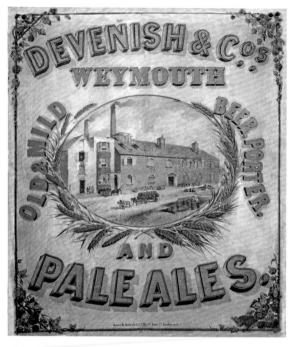

Advert for Devenish & Co.,
Weymouth.

Devenish Brewery.

Devenish tiled frontage on The
Royal Oak, Weymouth.

Two Devenish draymen 'getting their own back'.

Horse-drawn Devenish dray.

Beermat showing later Devenish branding.

concentrated at Redruth and, in 1986, Devenish merged with Michael Cannon's Inn Leisure plc. The Redruth Brewery was to close in 1994.

The old Devenish & Groves site became a leisure attraction after closure and now awaits further redevelopment. A visit and stroll around the old breweries and malthouses is recommended.

After eleven years, brewing returned to Hope Square in the summer of 1996. The Quay Brewery, set up by Giles Smeath, was able to use some of the old brewing kit and delivered its first brew with a flourish by horse-drawn dray. In 2004, the name changed to the Dorset Brewing Company. December 2010 saw production move from Brewers Quay to a new brewery at Crossways, thereby satisfying the increasing demand for its award-winning ales.

Just north of Weymouth, the Royal Standard at Upwey was renovated and reopened at Easter 2010. The renovation also included the installation of a small brewery, and DT Ales were born. The DT abbreviation is taken from the postcode for Upwey. Not so much a microbrewery as a nanobrewery, brewing commenced in August 2010. Under the management of Phil Anderson, two regular beers, DT3 and DT4, are produced. These have gone down well at the pub, which is always a pleasure to visit.

The old Devenish Brewery.

The first Quay Brewery delivery to the Kings Arms, Weymouth.

Right: Beer label for DT Ales, Upwey.

Below: The Royal Standard, Upwey.

Dorchester to Sherborne

From their beginnings at Brewers Quay in Weymouth as the Quay Brewery, the Dorset Brewing Company began brewing in earnest at their spring-fed, state-of-the-art Jurassic Brewhouse at Crossways in 2011. They renamed and rebranded in 2004 to take advantage of the designation of Dorset's Jurassic Coast as a World Heritage Site. In 2008, DBC took over Tom Browns in Dorchester, and the pub has effectively become their brewery tap. Along with its ever-popular permanent range, DBC brews seasonal beers and inventive monthly limited editions. Several secret brews are planned too.

To the south-west of Dorchester, the peaceful village of Martinstown, or Winterborne St Martin, was home to a brewery in the nineteenth century. The brewery was run from the 1840s by the Scutt family, who lived in what is now Old Brewery House, with the brewery located in buildings adjacent to the main house. George Scutt was the first brewer, followed by his son, George. By the time Groves of Weymouth acquired the brewery in 1889, it was run by William Francis Scutt, who was also at the Brewers Arms.

Above left: Advert for the Dorset Brewing Co., Weymouth.

Above right: 20 Years Anniversary pump clip, Dorset Brewing Company, Crossways.

Brewery House (left), Martinstown.

The Brewers Arms, Martinstown.

Onwards to the county town of Dorchester, where there has been a considerable range of brewing activity over the years – from brew pubs to an enormous cathedral of beer. Dozens of brewers have come and gone, including the Phoenix Brewery, which was behind the Phoenix Hotel in High East Street. The brewery was founded in the late eighteenth century by the Galpin family and stayed under their ownership for over a hundred years. When the brewery, along with its five pubs, was acquired by Groves of Weymouth from Galpin & Masters in 1898, it gave Groves valuable outlets in Dorchester.

Of course, Dorchester's most famous brewery was in Weymouth Avenue. Eldridge Pope & Co.'s history started when Charles Eldridge, then licensee of the Antelope Hotel, leased the Green Dragon Brewery in Durngate Street in 1837. His widow carried on the business in partnership with Alfred Mason after 1846, taking over the nearby Standish's Pale Ale Brewery in 1854. Edwin Pope purchased Mason's share in 1870 and was later joined by his brother Alfred to form the new company in 1874. Expansion was rapid as Edwin developed a range of beers to meet old and new tastes and Alfred secured a large tied estate and free trade by acquiring pubs in Dorset and along the railway line to the east of the town. Their new Dorchester Brewery next to the London & South Western Railway station was opened in 1881. This fine building featured in *The Brewers' Journal* and *The Engineer* and was to usher in a period of great prosperity. The company, incorporated in 1898, acquired breweries and tied houses in Poole, Cerne Abbas, Winchester, Twyford and Tisbury and opened a number of depots in this expanded area.

Advert for the Phoenix Hotel, Dorchester.

The Pale Ale Brewery arch, Dorchester.

Proposed design for Eldridge Pope's old brewery, Dorchester.

Profits fell in the recession of the 1920s and a fire that started in the hop store in 1922 destroyed the old brewery. Recovery, assisted by supplies of beer from the Wenlock Brewery in London, was swift. The Dorchester Brewery was rebuilt and re-equipped in just two years and completed its first brew in February 1925. Just prior to the fire, the company had adopted the huntsman for its posters and soon applied this trademark to its range of beers. The image was redesigned in 1935 as the old one was also used by Tetley of Leeds. The company added the Woolmington Brewery in Sherborne and some new pubs in the growing suburbs during this period. The Second World War passed more easily than the first and the post-war years saw the introduction of keg beers, canning for the supermarket trade and the introduction of lager after further modernisation of the brewery.

All seemed well in the 1980s, with popular brands such as Dorchester Bitter, Faust lager and the strongest beer brewed in Britain, Thomas Hardy's Ale, but company strategy fell short in the later years of the century. The brewery closed in 2003 after sale to a property company and is now part of the Brewery Square mixed-use development. In 2004 the pub estate was purchased by turn-around specialist Michael Cannon, who sold it to Marstons plc in 2007.

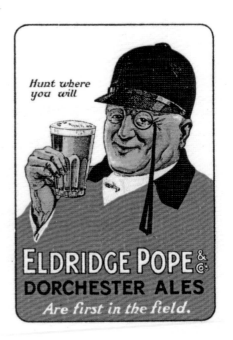

Above left: Fire drill at Eldridge Pope.

Above right: Eldridge Pope's Huntsman trademark.

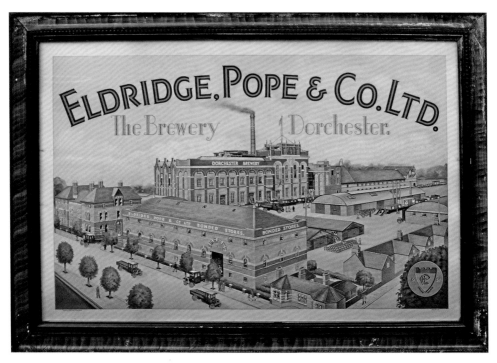

Advert for Eldridge Pope showing the new brewery.

First Prize & "Meader" Challenge Bowl. Boscombe Carnival. 1935.

Eldridge Pope float, Boscombe Carnival.

Eldridge Pope livery on The Britannia Inn, Portland.

ONE OF THE TRADITIONAL HUNTSMAN ALES BREWED BY ELDRIDGE POPE IN DORCHESTER

Left: Advert for Eldridge Pope's Dorchester Bitter.

Below: The Brewery Square development.

Still in Weymouth Avenue, on a corner of the old Eldridge Pope site, brewing has started again. This time it is on an altogether more modest scale in the shape of the Brewhouse & Kitchen pub. Part of a chain (with a similar pub in Poole and two more to open in Bournemouth and Southborne), Dorchester's Brewhouse & Kitchen is located in what was formerly The Station pub. The on-site brewery is particularly striking because of the gleaming copper vats. Beers brewed include Mayor of Casterbridge Porter and Judge Jeffreys Blonde.

Back across town to High East Street, the Chequers Hotel was a brew pub for the first part of the nineteenth century. Beer was brewed behind the premises by Thomas Tullidge and then by John Stevens. Renamed Tom Browns, brewing recommenced after a gap of around 140 years in 1987. As before, Simon Finch's Goldfinch Brewery was located in an outbuilding behind the pub. Sadly, Simon died in 2005. The Dorset Brewing Company took over the running of Tom Browns in 2008 and, true to the original recipes, they brew a selection of the Goldfinch beers off-site at Crossways.

Away from Dorchester, it is all change in the Piddle Valley at the Piddle Brewery. Set up in 1997 by Rob Martin and Paul Goldsack, and based at Piddlehinton, the business was sold in October 2014. The new owners instigated subtle changes to the branding, brewing equipment and beers in order to re-energise the Piddle Brewery, and allow it to compete in what is an increasingly crowded market in Dorset. As well as their core bitter, Piddle, their premium lager beer, No.1, is now proving popular with drinkers. A cider, Ciddle, was also launched and the beer range extended. Here's to a golden future.

Brewhouse & Kitchen, Dorchester.

Copper brewing vessels at the Brewhouse & Kitchen.

Above left: Tom Browns, Dorchester.

Above right: Flashmans Clout pump clip, Goldfinch Brewery, Dorchester.

Jon Lavers at the Piddle Brewery, Piddlehinton.

Advert for No. 1, Piddle Brewery.

A few miles further west, another rural village brewery was to be found at Sydling St Nicholas. The St Nicholas Brewery was founded in 1842 by the Newman family, who leased it to various brewers before selling it to Groves of Weymouth in 1905 when brewing ceased. The brewery building still stands as a private house, but with the loss of the top storey.

Still further west, at Melbury Osmond, the Melbury Oak Brewery was a very short-lived concern in the 1990s. After a few test brews locally, the venture was supplied with ale from outside Dorset. This factor, coupled with the varying quality of the beer, meant sales dried up.

Back to Cerne Abbas, the town that is overlooked by the Cerne Giant. Centuries ago, Cerne Abbas was famed for the quality of its ales. This brewing tradition was carried on in the nineteenth century by the Northover Brewery and several brew pubs. Brewing ceased in the 1890s, and only, possibly, a wall remains of the Northover Brewery that was behind 31 Long Street. The site of the brewery is now a small housing development, Abbey Court.

Further down Long Street, brewing at the New Inn probably continued into the early twentieth century. In 1920, the inn was acquired by Eldridge Pope, and is now an award-winning Palmers establishment.

Vic Irvine and Jodie Moore set up the Cerne Abbas Brewery in 2014. Vic's description of their brewery is as follows:

A modest brewery with giant integrity, we are brewers of eight delicious award winning beers. Not a sausage of quality will be compromised on the brewing of our beer. Brewery operations are moving to Cerne Abbas shortly. Will Best is growing our organic Maris Otter barley at Manor Farm, Godmanstone, in the Cerne Valley. We will be brewing with this directly after harvest. All of our bottles are available in Cerne Abbas Stores, and many other outlets run by nice people.

The old St Nicholas Brewery, Sydling St Nicholas. (Copyright the Mills Archive Trust – Alan Stoyel Collection)

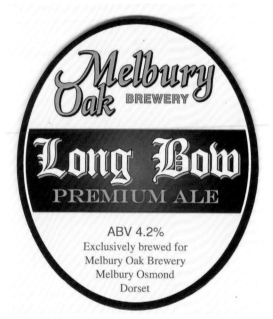

Long Bow pump clip, Melbury Oak Brewery, Melbury Osmond.

The old Northover Brewery house, Cerne Abbas.

The New Inn, Cerne Abbas.

Jodie Moore of the Cerne
Abbas Brewery.

Ale pump clip, Cerne Abbas Brewery.

Heading north, Stalbridge had two common brewers in the nineteenth century. In Church Hill, opposite the old Red Lion Hotel, the Taylor family owned a house with a small brewery attached, which closed in the 1880s. At the bottom of Gold Street, to the left when looking up the road, the white family operated a brewery and malthouse until the late 1870s. The brewing equipment was aunctioned off on 1879.

A couple of miles to the south-west, in the rural village of Stourton Caundle, beer has been brewed sporadically since 2011 at the Trooper Inn under the name of Blackmore Ales. Whether any of their beers are available or not, the award-winning Trooper is always a lovely pub to visit.

Advancing westwards, just outside Ryme Intrinseca, Chris Clark and Jane Reeves have been bitten by the brewing bug. Their Wriggle Valley Brewery began production in late 2014 in an outbuilding close to where they live. Their aim is to brew handcrafted beer, big on flavour. From tentative beginnings, they now brew three regular beers and two seasonal brews, including the rich Night Owl Porter. The beers are available in casks in a long list of local free houses, or in bottles from the brewery and an ever-growing number of stockists. Good health.

The old Taylor's brewery, Stalbridge.

The Trooper Inn, Stourton Caundle.

Chris Clark of the Wriggle
Valley Brewery, Ryme
Intrinseca.

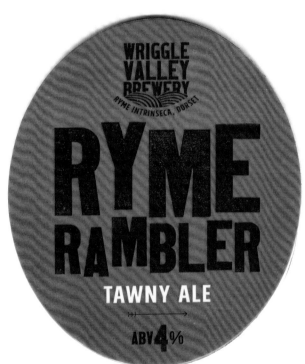

Ryme Rambler pump clip,
Wriggle Valley Brewery.

Back across the north Dorset countryside, there were as many as eighteen breweries in mid-nineteenth century Sherborne, and a number of independent maltsters. The origin of Woolmington's brewery at the top of Cheap Street is uncertain, but it was possibly started by John Withey, a brewer and maltster here in 1840. Isaac Woolmington was here in 1855 and the business was run by his widow Mary from 1873 until his sons took over in 1889. A small concern, it was acquired by Eldridge Pope in 1922, with eight pubs, and used as a depot and off-licence. The view of Sherbourne shows the Woolmington Hotel near the railway with a malthouse to the rear.

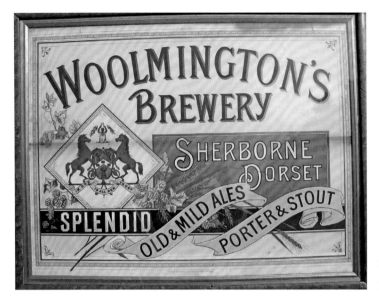

Advert for Woolmington's Brewery, Sherborne.

Woolmington Bros malthouse (right), Sherborne.

The Sherborne Brewery in Long Street was the largest in the town. Founded in 1796, it changed hands frequently after this until purchased by Abel Whittle of the Trendle Street brewery in 1856 and, as the Dorsetshire Brewery, passed to W. H. Baxter in 1887. The brewery was rebuilt in 1892 and incorporated as The Dorsetshire Brewery Ltd in 1926. It closed in 1951 when taken over, with seventy-eight pubs, by Brutton, Mitchell & Toms of Yeovil. Restored as apartments in the 1980s, the photograph on page 81 shows the malthouse with kiln chimneys as it was in 1973.

Brothers Stephen and Martin Walsh set up the new Sherborne Brewery in 2005, initially in an old yarn mill. They moved the brewery kit to behind their fish and chip shop, Abbey Friar, in Westbury in early 2007. By the Abbey Friar they have also opened Docherty's Bar and, more recently, the Cutty Sark Ale House, which are both outlets for their beer. After a pause in brewing, a major refurbishment will take place in 2016. The very welcome plan is to resume brewing later that year.

Above: The old Dorsetshire
Brewery, Sherborne.

Right: Beer label for the
Dorsetshire Brewery.

Above: Martin Walsh of the
Sherborne Brewery.

Left: Cheap Street pump clip,
Sherborne Brewery.

West Dorset

A brewery was established by the Gladwyn family in the small village of Litton Cheney as long ago as 1792. The peak output of the brewery was between 1860 and 1870 under James Randall Gladwyn, who was succeeded by Francis James Gladwyn. Brewing stopped around 1890.

Malting was carried out at nearby Barge's Farm, and the row of cottages opposite the brewery is still called Malters Cottages.

A survey in 1971 found the brewhouse with some of its equipment still *in situ*, including a 600 gallon cask in the cellar where the beer had been stored. Since then, the brewery has been converted into residential use.

The old Gladwyn's Brewery, Litton Cheney.

Malters Cottages, Litton Cheney.

Further west, Bridport's Old Brewery is now the only historic plant at work in Dorset. The site was purchased in 1794 by a partnership known as Samuel Gundry & Co. Bridport's seventeenth-century public brewery and malthouse has been mentioned in the introduction and this, together with a number of maltings and pub breweries, continued to provide for visitors and workers in this busy textile town up to this time. The Old Brewery, called Gundry, Downe & Co. from the 1830s, added the newly fashionable lighter Burton ales to the traditional range of table beer, porter and old vatted ales. In 1864 the business became the first in Dorset to adopt limited liability status as The Bridport Old Brewery Company Limited.

The new venture, however, proved a spectacular failure and the brewery was offered at auction by the liquidator in 1867, together with two malthouses, a newly built store house and forty-five freehold and leasehold tied houses. It was bought by Thomas Legg, a member of a well-known farming family from nearby Litton Cheney, who had previously become the owner of the New Brewery in the town. The business passed to his son Job in 1874. Job improved the brewery with the addition of a new waterwheel and improvements to the maltkilns and further added to its tied estate by taking over the Netherbury and Lyme Regis breweries. In 1892, Leggs owned thirty-five properties in the Bridport District and thirty-eight in the Bridport Borough licensing areas while his main rival, Crewkerne United Breweries, respectively held held nine and five in this area.

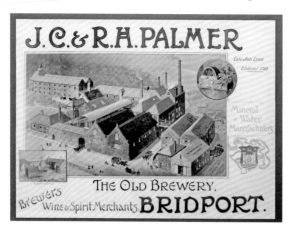

Advert for J. C. & R. H. Palmer, Bridport.

The Old Brewery, Bridport.

After Job's death in 1893, the brewery was purchased in 1896 by J. C. & R. H. Palmer, owners of a country brewery and farm in Odiham, Hampshire. Dorset was still suffering from a long depression in agriculture when their new venture began, but a combination of improvements to the brewery buildings and plant, the introduction of mineral waters and a bottling line resulted in extended product range – which included bottled lagers from 1904 – and improved financial performance. Further innovation, acquisitions and careful management of the tied estate and the business has ensured survival through the difficult years of wars and recessions in the twentieth century and the brewery, which became a private limited company in 1976, has maintained its traditions, independence and distinctive beers to this day. The listed Old Brewery, in part thatched, is one of Dorset's industrial treasures and a visit is a must for brewery enthusiasts.

Apart from the main breweries, Bridport had several pub brewers including the Bull Hotel in East Street and the Castle Inn in South Street. The Bull, established in the 1500s, was Bridport's premier coaching inn and beer was brewed there for centuries. The Knight family acquired the hotel in the nineteenth century with William George Knight last brewing on the premises in 1920.

At the more modest Castle Inn (on the left in the photograph of South Street on page 87) William Scadding was the last landlord to brew there for several decades until the pub closed in December 1914.

Advert for Palmers bottled beers.

Brewery drays at Palmers.

Above left: Pub sign at the Royal Oak Inn, Charmouth.

Above right: Advert for Palmers Pale Ale.

The waterwheel at Palmers Brewery.

Cleeves Palmer and John Palmer.

The Bull Hotel,
Bridport.

The Castle Inn
(left), South Street,
Bridport.

West of Bridport in the Dorset countryside, two historic brew pubs are still open today. At Symondsbury, the Ilchester Arms dates from the sixteenth century and had a brewhouse in the back yard. The business was acquired by Groves of Weymouth around 1900 and is now a Palmers pub.

The Shave Cross Inn, parts of which are 700 years old, was a busy stop-off for monastic visitors. Brewing took place in what is now the skittle alley, which is reputedly the oldest in the country.

In more modern times, John and Becky Whinnerah (pictured with their daughter Zoe) set up Art Brew in summer 2008. Located in a converted farm building in deepest north Chideock, Art Brew's aim was to experiment with flavours and ingredients to make extraordinary beer. Word quickly spread about beers such as Ginger & Chilli IPA and Blackberry Stout, and rave reviews followed. However, John and Becky have since relocated to north Devon, where Art Brew has had a welcome relaunch.

On the coast, larger-scale brewing in Lyme Regis faltered in the nineteenth century. John Sellers' brewhouse and malthouse in Broad Street, Gundry's Brewery stores and six inns burnt down in the Great Fire on 11 May 1844. Thomas Trafford's Lyme Regis Brewery closed in the 1860s. Brewing continued on a very small scale at the London Inn, latterly by the Stoward family, until around 1920.

The Ilchester Arms, Symondsbury.

The Shave Cross Inn.

Zoe, Becky and John
Whinnerah of Art Brew,
North Chideock.

Art Nouveau pump clip,
Art Brew.

The London Inn, Lyme
Regis.

Now part of the Town Mill complex, the Town Mill Malthouse dates back to the early eighteenth century. It was subsequently used by several small-scale brewers including John Davie, who brewed at the Golden Hart. The malthouse building was restored in 2010.

During the twentieth century, the Town Mill Malthouse housed a small electricity generating station. The former battery room at the right-hand end of the malthouse now houses the Lyme Regis Brewery.

Started in spring 2010 by a group of beer fanatics, the venture was originally called the Town Mill Brewery. Managing director Richard Surtees changed the name to the Lyme Regis Brewery in spring 2015 and launched a new beer, Dorset Pearl. Lyme Regis beers are widely available, including from the excellent brewery shop at Town Mill.

After a lengthy absence of beer producers, 2010 saw the launch of a second brewery in Lyme Regis. The Mighty Hop Brewery was set up in the summer of that year by Mark Jenkin, in his back garden. Mighty Hop concentrated on sales of bottled beer, which were well received. Expansion followed, still in the back garden, and Mark recruited internationally renowned brewster Emma Turner. However, Mighty Hop ceased brewing in May 2014, and the brewing kit was sold to the Brouwerij Den Drul in the Netherlands.

Back across to Maiden Newton, to the right of the photograph found on page 92, the townscape is overlooked by the brewery chimney. Established in the 1840s by Henry Cox and succeeded by Reynolds & Heathorn, brewing ceased in 1894. Now, the

The Town Mill Malthouse, Lyme Regis.

Town Mill Best pump clip, Town Mill Brewery, Lyme Regis.

Richard Surtees of the Lyme Regis Brewery.

Mark Jenkin of the Mighty Hop Brewery, Lyme Regis.

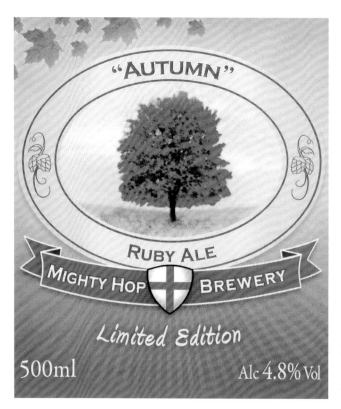

Left: Beer label for the Mighty Hop Brewery.

Below: Maiden Newton Brewery (right).

chimney has gone, but most of the brewery buildings are extant next to the Chalk & Cheese pub.

Further west at Mangerton Mill in Melplash, the Mangerton Brewery, or Netherbury Independent Brewery, was founded in 1860 by Thomas Rouning. The last to brew there, William Garland, went bankrupt, and the brewery and two pubs were acquired by Palmers of Bridport.

Close by in Netherbury, and not to be confused with the Netherbury Independent Brewery, the Knap Brewery was visible through the trees from the bridge at the bottom of the village. William Hoare was the brewer at the time of the eighteenth-century picture. The brewery was sold to Job Legg of Bridport in 1876 with five pubs.

The market town of Beaminster had several brew pubs rather than a common brewery. Brewers are listed at the White Hart from the seventeenth to the nineteenth centuries, during which time the White Hart was rebuilt twice.

Back to the present day, John Hosking and Amanda Edwards brewed their first Gyle 59 beer at Sadborow on 31 August 2013. With the focus on 'hazy crazy artisan beers', Gyle 59 brew a tremendous range of flavoursome and unfined ales.

In 2014, Emma Turner joined Gyle 59. Emma and Amanda are part of Project Venus, a group of brewsters who gathered to brew Venus Weizen at Gyle 59 on Halloween 2015. November 2015 saw the opening of the brewery bar and bottle shop. Cheers.

The old Netherbury Independent Brewery, Melplash.

The Knap Brewery, Netherbury.

The White Hart Hotel, Beaminster.